Trapped

Finding My Way out of Generational Curses

Part 1

Lanesha Allen

Trapped: Finding My Way out of Generational Curses Part 1

Printed in the United States of America

First Printing

ISBN: (pbk) 978-1-955148-51-1

ISBN: (ebk): 978-1-955148-52-8

A2Z Books Publishing Lithonia, GA 30058

www.A2ZBooksPublishing.net Manufactured in the United States of America A2Z Books Publishing has allowed this work to remain exactly as the author intended, verbatim.

Table of Contents

Introduction

Disclaimer: **I wrote this book years ago and this situation happened and now you will see why this book is titled Trapped!**

It's June 24th, 2022 and today started out like any normal day. Well for some it wouldn't be considered normal, since I was at my friend's funeral, but in my life, funerals come just like birthdays. Every time we looked around, it was someone else dying and another funeral to go to. I felt an eerie feeling when I woke up and to think about it, I've had this feeling for the last few days. With the way my life has been set up, even those feelings start to become normal, but this time that feeling was something that would change my life forever.

I was sitting inside my friend's funeral and this is how the Facetime went.

Me: Hello

My kids: Mom (Screaming), something bad happened.

Me: WHAT Happened? (Thinking someone broke something or they were fighting as usual.)

My Kids: GRANDMA'S DEAD

Me: WHAT (Screaming)

My Kids: GRANDMA'S DEAD

Me: OH MY GOD!!! WHAT…. (I had to run out of the funeral because I was so in shock, I thought I was dreaming).

But oh my, soon I will find out I am not dreaming. This is basically the story of my life. One bad thing happens after another.

I called my aunt and was told My mom was found in her house by the guy she was dating, on the kitchen floor. Come to find out she was dead for 2 whole days before he found her and what's even worse is they are saying it's a fentanyl overdose. So, I was thinking to myself, a fentanyl overdose? WHAT!! That doesn't even make sense, since all I ever thought she did was smoke a little weed. A fentanyl overdose just doesn't sound right… But once you get into my Life Story and how everything has unfolded, you'll see that almost nothing in my life made sense, from the time I was born.

This is Trapped: Finding My Way Out of Generational Curses

Generational Curse #1

Poverty

I never really understood life until it came to being hurt. It was like I was supposed to take it all in and wake up and be happy according to my family. Rolling with the flow became normal. Growing up on the East side of Detroit had its ups and downs, especially coming from a financially stable but mentally dysfunctional family. I never thought that I would be a runaway, but I have been running away from home damn near my whole fuckin life because of generational curses that have been passed down from my family onto me. Circumstances that have chewed me up, swallowed me whole, and then spit me the fuck out repeatedly. Drugs, addiction, overdoses, and murder amongst so many other terrible things are my story on dealing with generational curses and unfortunately for me, it does not get any better from there. I experienced all the luxuries that a child could dream of besides structure and love. I am guessing with the good come bad but in my case, there were plenty of bad to come. As far as I can remember honestly everything was stable besides the fact that there were no male figures present which is confusing for a child who does not understand how she can identify father figures amongst her peers but hers was nowhere to be found, go figure. Because of that it left my mother Princess to pick up both parenting roles and to raise her child alone. The consensus across America seems to be that the so called 'deadbeat' fathers leave because they do not care anymore. ***Why do fathers leave their children?*** Fathers do not simply abandon their families out of laziness or lack of love; they leave because they feel unworthy. Just maybe that was the case for me; I really cannot tell you why there was an absence of my father in my life. I have heard my mom's side and it does not make sense to me. It never held a major effect on my life because how can you want something you never had. Seems like my mother was searching for love as well but then again, it is kind of confusing to me because the men that she was with over the years I took notice to the fact that she was very controlling towards them. I am the only child so that tells you she was not up for any bullshit. Princess and my dad Ant did not last long. He had some drug issues and family issues that she was not willing to deal with, so she distanced herself and me from him. She always says she did not want any kids and that my dad made her have me and she felt bad for him. Sounds crazy as hell when you are bringing a child in this world without a strategic plan for that child's future but when you think about it so many people do the exact same thing. Basically, they are setting their child or children up for failure. ***What I have learned from life is removing a man from the home destroys a lot of structure from the household. Most black women seem to feel like if a man doesn't financially help then he is useless in a home which is immoral.*** But then again so many young black girls grow up in single mother households and they watch their mothers struggle to make ends meet. They watch their mothers struggle to get by and they even watch their mother's attempt to date different men who for the most part are deadbeats just like their fathers are. That gets plenty of black women to believing just like most of their mother's teach them that if a man isn't doing for you financially, he's worthless. Do not get me wrong, finance is a major factor in sustaining a strong household, but it is not the only factor. ***Every child needs their father's love and what so many single mothers teach their children is that they can do everything by themselves without a man.*** It destroys the psyche of a young girl or boy.

Of course, the man is the provider but providing consists of many other things that are unbelievably valuable to a woman and child's life and future. By removing the man away from the home takes away leadership qualities that only a father can provide and show to their child. My dad was on some bullshit because I have heard stories about things he did. For instance, my uncle who I will soon introduce said he went to deliver him some narcotics and my dad grabbed them and took off running. That was some real dope fiend shit if you ask me. And the fact that he was never around me made me feel like he did not care for me at all. I was never bitter though; he was a cool dude when I stayed with him for a couple of months. I just feel like she should have made better judgements before she conceived me. I guess watching her choices will soon follow me in the worst way. It is all sweet and games when you think the child is all cute and blind but really, they are learning every detail of your life that will ultimately affect their future. Wondering why your kid is going against all the things you want them to know and feel but instead they have been just watching your life to use it as an excuse to fuck their life up. But it's really up to the parent to present the child with a proper upbringing for their future. Other than that, I witnessed my mom having a lot of male friends. She had a couple of relationships, but they did not last long. Her tolerance level was low. I mean she was always telling them what to do and being very controlling. She did not embrace her femininity at all; she likes to be in control of things. My mom is the take charge type of woman which is not good at all for a thriving household. And what adds injury to insult is that it seems like only the black race is like this, our women are not submissive at all. Especially in the times we are in now. I am terrified of this new generation and so on. So anyway, my mom always liked to cut the grass and do other things a man should do, which I never understood by her having so many brothers around her. It seems like she was a bit hardcore to me, but with a cute lady side to her. Do not get twisted though she is very classy. Her favorite perfume was always an obsession so wherever she went she smelt just like a bottle of it. She walked with a twist, she has always been prissy, and she had very long hair. She was big on keeping herself up. Clear skin, very pretty and she took care of herself so well that she never appeared to be of her true age at all. From cucumber peels over her eyes every morning to Aloe Vera blanketing her skin every single day, when it came to personal appearance my mother did not play around. She also felt that she did not need a man still, go figure. The same generational curse that plagued others of my same bloodline was continuing in my life, occurring right before my young eyes. But I was blind to the fact that I was even included in this toxic upbringing. In my earlier years I noticed that Princess was very disconnected with affectionate love that we all as young women need. I yearned for her affection, but her affection was invisible. Her affectionate love came through dolling me up and making me look nice. For instance, my hair and clothes stayed laid to the point that it was a fashion show. Every time I turned around, she was saying "pose Nesha take this picture." There were no hugs and kisses included with the gifts, only strict lessons, and hard beatings with no explanation, which every child needs following discipline. Everything came with a cost meaning I used to have that mentality thinking that buying your kids nice expensive clothing and making sure they are fresh is what a good parent should do, but it is not. It leads to entitlement and materialism. I am not saying children should not have nice things but simply just making sure they understand the value of things is very important as well. As early as 7 years old I started to rebel against things that I thought was right and wrong which is unethical which was crazy because, in disciplinary areas of my life my mother ruled with an iron fist. She would beat the crap out of me. Her favorite thing to say was "shut up before you be picking your teeth up off the ground," and she was not just talking either. Every beating I got felt as bad as someone yanking a tooth out of my mouth. My mother did not have a motherly presence, so her approach to me at times was sometimes wrong. She always showed possessive love, and from stories I have heard about her and her mother's relationship kind of reminds me of the one I have with her. She was very disconnected with her mother, which explains why she treated me the way she did. I cannot really give too many details about my grandmother and grandfather's relationship but what I do know is my grandmother used to drink a lot and make a fuss. My grandfather whose name was Lawrence was stressing my grandmother the hell out with his lifestyle and how he was a ladies' man. And whatever other issues they had. My mother Princess's heart was with her father Lawrence, and she was in love with him. He gave her so much love and spoiled her ass rotten. Lawrence draped her in all the nicest clothing, and she traveled to many places and experienced his extravagant lifestyle with him. She lived in Cali on Melrose next door to the man who created Famous Amos cookies so that tells you she was a very fortunate child. Where he went is where she went. I guess the gifts from her father led her to overlook all the fucked-up shit that was going on in her young life. I mean I know he loved her, but I just truly believe that she just didn't get the full life of how a child is supposed be raised. Some may have seen the life that I lived growing up as paradise but for me in the years to come would show that it was nothing but a living hell. I was oblivious to the fact that the neglect of love was the destruction of a nation's upbringing. But then again, I was a child lost in the thoughts of what ifs. My life was forming into a world wind of uncertainty and an unimaginable feeling of abandonment. As a young child growing up, I quickly realized that there was also a necessary understanding for me to stay strong because honestly it was rough. Poverty was an everyday thing where others that lived in places like West Bloomfield and Rochester Hills did not experience the hardships that me and my family experienced. Not financially but as far as structure is concerned there was an absence of it. Simply money was never an issue, but communication and values were always issues that plagued my family and if you ask me if you have a poor mindset that leads to poverty. Just because you are winning for the moment does not mean you will win forever. Soon I would be in charge of another life's destiny. We as human beings never understand that the actions of our own reflect on every living and thriving thing around us and as an unguided blind young female, I would soon learn that there was an unparalleled line between what I thought was right vs. what actually was right. It was never honestly explained to me. Frequent flights to Chicago all alone at a tender age to visit my grandma Lisa and my uncle Allen who was brutally slain in a gangland style murder still sits with me. Grandma Lisa was my grandfather Lawrence's last child's mother who I was very close to. Trips to Chicago were cool besides the fact that my uncle Allen used to scare me with Freddy Krueger and Candyman. He used to lock the bathroom door and turn the lights off and made me say

Candyman in the mirror. It was straight torture. He is the reason I have anxiety issues. Allen was out of control. He kept an attitude with his face always turned up. But then again, he was going through the same shit I was going through. He had every pair of Jordans you can think of. My grandfather died while he was younger so maybe his actions came from having an absent father. Just so you know it takes two to raise a child and unfortunately for my family and so many other black families we don't get that two-parent household that we need. How it is supposed to be is that the mother shows love while the father shows discipline. Every child need love but every child also needs discipline so the two are supposed to balance each other out. What is happening and what has been happening in single parent household's particularly single mother households is too much love is being given to bad children and they're not being disciplined for their bad actions. The excessive amount of love they are being given without ever truly being disciplined for their bad behavior is why so many young men and young girls grow into criminals in their adult years. See my Uncle Allen was fucked up mentally and I know him not having a father to guide him and discipline him in his earlier years destroyed his adult years. The story of my uncle Allen that was told to me is that he joined a gang, and he was trying to get out of the gang, so they killed him. They stabbed him thirty-two times and supposedly cut his penis off. I do not even know if that is all the way true, but he definitely had a horrible death. I remember vividly it was like he got rewarded for his bad behavior but on the up and up I really enjoyed being around them. My favorite was to walk to Fuddruckers with him.

That is why I love cheese so much. He did not play about his cheese loaded on a burger. It just seemed like my life was destined to be what it was without me knowing that the Lord works in mysterious ways. Thank you, God, for the many blessings you have given me. Back in Detroit as far as my schooling went I did okay. I really did not have problems with my schooling in my young years. The only thing I hated was the snow up to my knees in the wintertime. My great aunt, whose name was Aunt Fay, was also a real pentacle in my life as far as structure is concerned. She was a dental surgeon, so if you got into an accident and your teeth were damaged, she would fix it. She had her own dental office. I used to spend a lot of time with her growing up. She used to take us to church, and we spent nights at her house. She was cool besides the fact that she had a house full of cats and one day one of them attacked me. I was a little devious because I pulled cool cat tail and the reaction of that cat left me frightened still to this day. I absolutely do not like cats. My Aunt Fay had us playing instruments. She taught us how to play the flute. She had two sons that died in the Detroit River from trying to save someone else. RIP Rod and Curt. As far as family is concerned, I would give the credit to her as far as accomplishing sustainable goals. She did not play about our dental hygiene. We spent a lot of time at her dental office. Although I did not get a chance to meet my grandparents Lawrence and Dorothy, I was able to meet my great grandparents, but I do not have much memory of them besides visiting their big house on Seyburn where they lived. All I remember is the long spiral steps. That was my favorite thing to slide down those steps. My great grandfather Joe and my great grandmother Charity were very hard workers who owned the Allen's Ice cream parlor on the east side and a couple of liquor stores. I have heard before he moved to Detroit where he also ran illegal moonshine selling liquor. That all changed and he became legal. I was told they were sweet people who were just trying to make an honest living. My Great Grandmother Dorothy was basically a housewife who made sure Joe and the family was taking care of. I do have this memory of Joe taking me to Belle Isle to go Deer hunting. We killed a deer and put it on top of the car to eat but every time I tell someone that story, they tell me that it is not true. My great grandparents had a couple of children, one of them is Aunt Fay and a couple of uncles who I was super cool with, but they are all dead now. Uncle Richard was one of my favorites. My grandfather Lawrence on the other hand was probably the knucklehead of their crew, which you know is my mother's father. The glimpses of love that she would show me were pure, but I am guessing that the hardcore lifestyle that she was used to never truly allowed her to know what showing love to the ones you should love the most really meant. All the money in the world with no morals equals disaster.

L.A TIPS: CHILDREN WHO LIVE IN URBAN OR RURAL AREAS OFTEN FIND THEMSELVES IN A PRECARIOUS SITUATION. DUE TO EXTREME POVERTY, THEY CAN BE EXPOSED TO DANGER AND VIOLENCE, ETC. FAMILY EMPOWERMENT IS THE FIRST KEY TO SOLVING THE PROBLEM, MAKING BETTER

CHOICES, TAKING SACRAFICES TO MAKE SURE YOUR CHILD IS NOT EXPOSED TO THE BEHAVIOURS THAT HAPPENS AROUND THEM IN THOSE AREAS.

L.A TIPS: PARENTS SHOULD ALWAYS TEACH MORAL VALUES BY BEING THEIR ROLE MODELS. TO MAKE YOUR CHILDREN RESPONSIBLE HUMAN BEINGS THINGS SHOULD BE TAUGHT, SUCH AS HONESTY, LOYALTY, RESPECT, SELF RELIANCE, SELF DISAPLINE, PATIENCE, KINDNESS, GRATEFULNESS.

Generational Curse #2

Materialism

From my understanding, the honest legacy my great-grandparents wanted to leave behind was demolished by Lawrence and my uncle Old Dude. Joe and Charity worked very hard to provide a life for their family. Joe ran an illegal moonshine business in another state. He ended up moving to Detroit to become legit by owning a couple of liquor stores and of course the infamous Allen's Ice Cream Parlor. I was told they were sweet people who were just trying to make an honest living. However, Lawrence had a notorious reputation in Detroit Michigan. *Why is it that in black culture legacies are not left behind for future generations?* Joe and Charity paved the way for us to have a good life but somehow the streets got the best of my granddad.

Everyone in Detroit knew who my family was because of their luxurious lifestyle and menacing behavior. I mentioned my family because Lawrence was just the knucklehead, his brother, and his sons and other family members ran this operation from my understanding. My grandparents didn't move as their son did. However, the hustle mentality was injected into my whole family. Although we seek validation through material things, we still were natural-born hustlers. Whether its dope dealing or hustling or even working a job. Lawrence started living a wildlife in his later years. Don't ask me how this all became because from what I know he was a good kid! He ended up graduating high school, then attended college and worked an honest job until he met up with some cartel members, and from then on, he was turned on to the drug game. Once he saw fast money he never turned back. I guess going from slaving forty hours plus every week didn't beat making twice that money in a quarter of the time. All these things occurred in the midst of Detroit being the murder capital. In the 60's the city suffered the deadliest riot known up until that point. My grandfather turned into a drug lord and ran a very intense operation in no time. That explains why he draped my mother and everyone around him in the finest clothes and he brought them all the luxurious items anyone could ever ask for. The expensive cars, jewelry, and clothes gravitated to him and all those around him that he cared for because the money appeared seemingly out of nowhere for him and it continued to pour in for a very longtime. I've been told so many stories how my grandfather and his crew were cutting people's fingers off in my great-grandfather's store and them selling drugs out of the garbage trucks. With plenty of money came plenty of unlimited power and my grandfather took full advantage of it. People would say in front of the world that they have pride and dignity so much so that they would never accept drug money from anyone. "But behind closed doors, while they're living damn near in poverty or they're just struggling to pay the bills they will rethink that so-called pride and dignity that they have." Mailmen, garbage men, truck drivers, and so many blue-collar workers were on my grandfather's payroll accepting money that they would never make in a decade working for the companies that they worked for. My grandfather was a huge fan of Italian crime family movies, and his idols were all rich drug dealers who lived extravagant lifestyles. He wanted to mirror their lives by any means necessary and he ended up doing just that in real life. Those who betrayed my grandfather either ended up with their fingers being sliced off or they ended up dead in allies across the city. He knew that messages had to be sent to make sure that no one would dare disrespect him and he continuously sent messages over and over again. Even as fiends dropped dead left and right all over the city that didn't stop my grandfather from dealing as much drugs as the cartel would send his way. Overdose after overdose in broad daylight by the same drugs purchased from my grandfather was common all throughout the city but the demand for more drugs was continuously rising and that explains why his empire continued to grow all over Detroit. There were plenty of lives lost because of my grandfather's drugs but as I've heard from other people his old saying was "if he wasn't the one supplying the drugs to the people someone else would be doing that exact same thing." I guess that's how he slept at night or quite frankly I guess he truly didn't give a fuck. In his mind, he must've felt as though if you buy drugs from him or any of his drug pushers you know the deadly consequences that are possible to come from your actions. If I'm not mistaken there were even police officers on my grandfather's payroll who were paid to turn a blind eye to him and his crew. Nearly two decades of destruction took place in the city all because of the greed of my grandfather who didn't slow down at all with his drug dealing. In fact, he kept the pedal to the meddle because he enjoyed all the luxuries that came with him making so much money and, he had a lot of kids and plenty of family members to take care of. My grandfather Lawrence was known all throughout the city because his suits cost thousands of dollars each. He dressed like money, and he attracted plenty of it to him. He even wore bellbottoms and a halter top. I guess you can be a gangster and still dress fashionably without being looked at funny back in the day. But in the drug game, there's always consequences for your actions and for him, he experienced plenty of consequences for his activity. Years before he took over the drug game in the city my grandfather met my grandmother and had my mom and two boys. Then he ended up divorcing my grandmother only to get remarried and then he had another son with her. For whatever reason that did not work out he met Grandma Sarah and had my uncle Allen who used to scare me. My grandfather was a rolling stone, and he lived that way. He was a lady's man who was loved by so many women. His confidence, swag along with his money and power attracted so many women to him and he sure didn't decline any of their advances towards him. His playa ways were ultimately what ended his marriage to my grandmother. My grandfather cheated on my grandmother with his second wife, and I heard this story about him and the lady being in Allen's ice cream parlor and my grandmother was outside shooting at the store. He just kept his playa ways going all throughout his second marriage and although his second wife didn't like it, there was nothing that she could do about it. The number of lives lost in that store because of my grandfather's actions isn't even countable. So many demons rested in that store and karma was headed in his direction a million miles an hour. He could sense it. He knew that trouble was coming, which is why he sat up in that store all night with a shotgun resting on his lap and several of his men with guns walking all throughout the store. His crew's loyalty lied with him because he took care of them all financially. He made sure they all had a place to live of their own and he made sure all their bills were paid just like he did for our family. He never valued money and that is a generational curse that has fallen into my lap, and it started long before I was even born. The value of a dollar never meant a thing to him and that is why so many people gravitated to him whether they were genuine or not. The sound of the store glass shattering sound off as a bunch of bullets flew right into the store which struck a few of his men killing a couple of them instantly. My grandfather returned fire at the vehicle passing by unloading rounds of bullets into his parent's store that he tarnished the legacy of. He shot back repeatedly as the car sped away but the immense amount of blood that spilled all over the place caught his attention as the sound of sirens sounded off in the distance. It was on that night he knew that the people closest to him weren't safe and he needed to beef up his security team. Grandma Sarah and his newest-born son were on the first flight from Detroit to Chicago in the matter of hours as he sent a few of his men over to his ex-wife's home. My grandmother reminded him that if he continued to play in the streets acting as if he was invincible, he would surely find out that he was not. He had no choice but to hear her rant on and on about his terrible life choices but in order to silence her like always he reached into his pocket and pulled out a handful of money. He handed it to her and told her that she wouldn't see him for a while but no matter what, she would be protected. My grandmother despised him even more after that, once she found out that he moved Sarah to Chicago but left his old family back in Detroit to possibly face the evils that he's created. My grandfather left Detroit for no more than three days before he returned once he was sure that Sarah was settled in comfortably in Chicago with his newborn son. But trouble remained because my mother and one of her best friends were kidnapped because of his actions. One story I heard about her past took place around that time. From what I heard it had something to do with the backseat of a yellow taxicab and my mother being stripped naked and kidnapped along with her best friend. It all happened because there were people looking for my grandfather and because they couldn't get to him, they went after the closest person to him. Fortunately, my mother and her best friend ended up getting away. That situation shook my mother to her core and my mother and her father ended up moving away to Cali for a little bit. They moved to Melrose and somehow ended up moving into a home right next door to the man who created the Famous Amos cookies. They ended up moving back to Detroit after some time but there was hell to pay for a lot of people who were enemies of my grandfather. The next two weeks were the deadliest for the city of Detroit. It was the worst the city had ever experienced in its history. Bodies dropped and the streets were completely shaken by my grandfather who returned to Detroit even more heartless than he originally was. He didn't have a conscience and he had no nonsense for the bullshit any further because someone came for him, and they came and kidnapped his daughter. As far as I know he ended up meeting up with the cartel to supply him even more drugs than ever before. He lowered the prices of the drugs that he sold that ultimately wiped out all of his competition and in no time, he became the biggest drug dealer in the city. He profited even more in doing so because he went from getting more drugs from the cartel weekly to damn near every other day. His competitors either relocated to a different part of the state, to a new state or they filled out applications to work for my grandfather, imagine that. The money poured in like rain in the eye of a hurricane. Even though all the bullshit that my grandfather ended up putting my grandmother through she still loved him dearly. In fact, she never recovered from that situation. It explained why she drank so much. I heard stories about my grandmother drinking a lot and always being in a bad mood because he was stressing her out. He left her high and dry. Never did she believe that he would leave her only to remarry another woman in no time and that's what he did. My grandmother never truly had the time to cope. She didn't have any time to deal with the pain of her husband leaving her for another woman. He left her with children to raise and truly besides the money that she was always given by him she didn't offer much to her own children besides that. She was always stressed out and going through terrible mood swings because of him. I know deep down she never got over him and she was never able to move on to someone else because of the unlimited love that she had for him. She did remarry someone that my mother hated and deep down inside I believe my grandmother was never truly happy with her new husband. She was very disconnected from her children, especially from my mother. It was to the point that my mother didn't want to be around her own mother because the love was never there. Instead, my mother was always around her father, and he was always with other women so I can only imagine the kinds of things my mother witnessed growing up. The life my mother grew up in wasn't normal at all and that's why in so many ways I do forgive her for the lack of love and affection that she showed me through my upbringing because she never received that love and affection. Certain things in life must be taught and that's something that should've been taught to my mother and because it wasn't how could she teach that or show that to anyone? When I think about it, it explains why she didn't have that motherly affection with me because she didn't receive it herself. I know that my mother loved her mom, but my mother's heart really lied with my grandfather. He was her go-to person. She was in love with her dad. It still broke her heart if you talked about her dad whether it was good or bad, tears will be dropping from her eyes with anyone mentioning her father's name. Even up until the very end of my mother's life it still broke my mother's heart that her father was no longer alive. She cried like he died just a day ago and *Now I can relate I really miss her*. He was the person who named her Princess and that's what everyone called her. Dysfunction entered my mother's life as she was a child and dysfunction continued to follow my mom up until the very end. She never grew up in a normal home with both her mother and father. She's been rough around the edges all her life because of the lack of love she received from her mother and the toughness she was exposed to by her father. Although he treated her like his little angel, he treated anyone disloyal to him with an iron fist. He was a no-nonsense kind of man and that is something my mother witnessed nearly her whole life. Her idol didn't put up with anyone's crap and that's exactly how he told her to be and that's exactly how she has been nearly her whole life. My mom isn't very feminine at all. She's the take-charge type. She likes to change tires and cut the grass which are all things that women aren't known for doing. She has been very dependent on herself nearly her whole life and that never changed even after she had me her only child. She always had men around her that could do stuff for her, but she would always do things a man was supposed to do because she never felt like she needed a man to do anything for her. Which is so insane to me. Her father would always tell her that she didn't need a man and that stuck with her all this time. My mother is kind of like gangster and a lady mixed into one. She might take on the feminine role for a man that she cares greatly for but once that man messes up with her all hell breaks loose and that gangster tucked away inside of her like a bullet in a gun explodes at that very moment. She didn't play any games and she's not to be messed over by anyone. While in her presence I did my very best to stay on my best behavior because I knew what would come my way wouldn't be good for me or my behind if I dared acted out of character. That belt would hit me so fast and so hard I would never see it coming and that's if I was lucky. When I wasn't lucky it could be a shoe, a mop, a wide stick or whatever she could get her hands on just to inflict pain on me for acting up. My mother didn't play that when it came to disrespect, and she didn't tolerate it from anybody at any time because her father wouldn't allow her to. The stories I've heard about my mother's past is traumatizing. I believe it's another reason why she always deflects love. It's like love tries to find its way into her heart but she just swats it away like a fly every single time. I don't think she knows what it means to let your guard down to anyone ever. She may have cared deeply about someone, but I don't ever think she ever allowed herself to truly give her all to anyone including me her only child. All the trauma and hard-core lifestyle she lived as a child explains it all but there's still so much about her life that I didn't know. I feel bad for her based on what I do know about her childhood, but I can only imagine what she's been through along her journey. With her being the only daughter of the city's biggest drug dealer came with plenty of glitz and glamour but I'm quite sure it came with a tremendous amount of hell that can't be explained with words. For my family's generational curses, it began with my grandfather who hit the lottery in his eyes when he became friends with the biggest cartel on the East side. For him making money came fast. Everyone had nice clothes. All his siblings and his sibling's kids were well taken care of. They all took trips everywhere. I mean you name the place, and they went there you name the great adventures, and they did it all. If my family did anything they spent money like it was nothing and they enjoyed everything in life that money could buy. One thing though above all is that my grandfather didn't teach anyone the true value of money because as fast as he was making the money, he was spending the money just as fast while making even more money. He showed it with his actions and everyone around him could see that money wasn't a damn thing to him ever. My grandfather replaced love with money. Instead of showing anyone true affectionate love he did it instead with his wallet. That was his way of showing the ones he cared for that he loved them. It wasn't hugs and kisses it was all about splurging on them just to show them exactly how much they mean to him. I'm guessing the more money he spent on a person meant the more he cared for that person and that's probably why my mother had every doll, all the latest clothes, and everything else her heart ever desired.

His power grew so great that he had the streets shook nonstop. He grew so comfortable that he called for his new wife to come right back to Detroit. But when someone thinks they're on top of the world and they're doing nothing but wrong the Lord finds a way to bring that person right back down to reality in a heartbeat. No more than a week passed by after his new wife returned that he started receiving death threats from rival gangs. Although my grandfather thought he was invincible, he knew that he could only do so much to keep his wife and their child protected. So, he decided to send them far away this time and he sent them straight to Atlanta. One would think that a person who's faced the grim reaper on countless occasions would eventually change their ways, but my grandfather wasn't that way. He continued his drug dealing path and he continued buying people's love and affection with gifts and endless amounts of money. My mother for one benefited greatly from his big heart towards his loved ones. He continued showering her with gifts even though the relationship he had with my mother's mother was over. The money came in too easily and he had a kind heart for giving to the ones he cared for the most. Even though that was the case he was still well known in the streets for being evil. Eventually, he was murdered and left in the trunk of his car for 2 days dead in front of his parent's driveway.

My family became a bunch of rich well-dressed misfits who broke a lot of laws and got arrested repeatedly. We all knew that we needed love but none of us ever figured out just how to show that love to each other. Imagine being raised in a broken home but being gifted every gift that you could ask for. You become a spoiled brat who resents anyone that can't give you whatever you ask for and that's a major reason why my family has suffered so much over the years. We never had any values. We just had plenty of money and that's a generational curse that still affects us all, especially me. Because I know for a fact that I inherited that gene from my family. I waste money like it's trash and my values and principles weren't right then and I'm still battling all of that now in my older life. The ice cream parlor my great-grandparents left behind for my family was eventually lost because we didn't value it. Instead, the street money, the fast money was the only thing my family valued. If my great grandparents were alive to see what my family eventually became, they both probably would've died of broken hearts because how they raised their children just isn't how they turned out to become as they got older.

L.A TIPS: MANY PARENTS ARE NOT VERY WISE WITH MONEY AND DON'T MODEL HEALTHY FINANCIAL RESPONSIBILITY TO THEIR CHILDREN. WHILE SOME PARENTS CATER TO A CHILDS EVERY WHIM AND FANCY, OTHERS ARE EXCESSIVELY STINGY. SOME CONTINUOUSLY OVERSPEND AND LIVE BEYOND THEIR MEANS, WHILE OTHERS KEEP FINANCES A SECRET AND PRETEND LIKE DAYS DON'T MATTER. IT LEADS TO CHILDREN NOT KNOWING THE REAL VALUE OF MONEY, WHICH TRICKLES DOWN TO THEM DEVELOPING BAD HABITS THAT WILL CARRY INTO THEIR ADULTHOOD. SO, IT'S VERY IMPORTANT TO TEACH YOUR CHILDREN ABOUT THE IMPORTANCE OF MONEY AND WHAT IT TAKES TO HAVE AND KEEP.

Generational Curse #3

Addiction

*A*ddiction is something that's not easy to deal with. For many people, addiction invades and destroys their lives along with the lives of the people they cherish the most. It becomes a habit that seeks and terminates anyone that comes in its path and unfortunately, it sought out my family and destroyed so many of us. Poverty hit my family hard but when the money came, materialism struck my family like gold dropping into the home of a poor family. As bad as those two generational curses were to my family, I would say nothing was worse than addiction. Let me take you through a little journey right quickly. My mother wasn't close with that many people and that includes me, her own daughter. The love and affection were never there, or at least I never saw it that way. One of those people who saw her love was Ashley, one of my mother's closest friends who ended up moving to Atlanta from Detroit. I remember one evening after coming home from school just days before Spring Break, my mother had a few suitcases packed for me and her. She didn't tell me where we were going, she just told me that we were leaving town for a while. But little did I know that we were going on the first flight from Detroit to Atlanta to visit my mother's best friend Ashley. Ashley and my mother hung out a lot back in Detroit, but Ashley was dealing with her own relationship issues. Her husband was a drunk and was very abusive to her. I would constantly see her show up at my mother's house back in Detroit with bruises all over her arms and neck and sometimes even with a black eye or two. Her husband was so abusive to her, to the point that she knew that running away from him was her only option and that's what she did. I remember that trip to Atlanta with my mother because of how happy she appeared to be for the first time in such a long time. She seemed excited and just relieved to be in a new place with new people. Being far away from the drama that was in Detroit brought calmness over my mother that she never let go of. She and I moved out of the city straight to Atlanta in 1997, just after the Olympics. I remember when our flight landed in Atlanta my mother knew that it was going to be a fresh start in a brand-new city for her. *But with any good always comes some bad and that level of bad can never be determined until it happens.* A few months after we moved to Atlanta my mother's best friend who convinced her to move to Atlanta was shot in the head five times by that same abusive husband who found out exactly where she moved to. My mother was doing so well up until that point. This incident devastated her, and it showed. But for my family, it always seems that the good times only last for a short period of time. She fell into a depression and that wasn't good for her or me. My mother at that time just wasn't in the right frame of mind to take care of me or even herself so she had me sent back to the city to spend some time with my father. When I arrived in Detroit it was my uncle Old Dude who came to pick me up and quickly my excitement went away. My dad was busy from the moment I made it back to Detroit. He was always running the streets figuring out more and more ways to get to the money. In other words, he didn't have much time for me but that's another story. *I know that he loved me dearly, it's just that money was more important to him.* It came to the point that he had to sacrifice his own happiness in order to make those happy around him. I know that he must've hoped that his loved ones saw that but how my family operated, there was no way in hell that they thought that way. It sucked though because my father did most of his hustling to support his family. It's just how life goes, *I guess. You can go above and beyond for other people that you care for the most, but people are so stuck on themselves and their own problems that they may never realize any of that.* Anyway, I ended up spending most of my visit with my uncle Old Dude which was totally against my mother's wishes. She clearly told my dad to not let me go over there but he didn't listen to anything she had to say, which explains why they never worked out. I ended up staying with my uncle the whole summer while my mom was in Atlanta. I stayed with my Uncle

Old Dude and his wife and their two kids who became my favorite cousins. *When I say life happens suddenly and unexpectedly life happens in an instant.* During that summer I lost my virginity to a guy who was much older than I was. He bust my cherry and I remember it like it was yesterday. I remember that day also because I remember on the news it was about 2pac dying and the guy who I was having sex with jumped up from the bed after I started bleeding. Plus, he was devastated that 2pac was killed. That day plays out in my head over and over again, I just can't get over it. I remember when it was all over, and I had to walk back bloody as hell back to my uncle's home. I was terrified that he would see me, but as luck would have it, my favorite girl cousin was at home waiting on me. But as good as that sounds, it was anything but that because my uncle had this burglar bar door at the front and back door, and it stayed locked. There was only one way around that gate and that was to crawl underneath it so that's what I did that night along with my cousin who waited outside for me. *This wasn't the first time we crawled under that gate to get to the basement or to escape from his house from the back of the house.* We were young, dumb, and grown, and if anything, we were just trying to live our lives, so we did what we had to do that summer to have some fun. My uncle didn't play around with us at all. He even had a big ass steel jail door at the front door just to make sure no one would try to break in. On that night though I told my cousin where I was going before I left and when I got back, she was at the gate waiting on me. We threw those all-white Nike joggers in the washer so fast before my uncle could catch me. She definitely was my ride-or-die. It was weird because after we did all of that craziness, we ended up sitting down in her room to watch power rangers. That show was our shit back then and I didn't miss an episode. During that summer I also experienced my uncle and aunt both doing heroin really bad. My uncle was a user and a dealer of heroin whereas my aunt was just the housewife who took care of the kids and got high as hell whenever she could. Addiction ran wild through my family for years, but that summer was the first time I truly saw it up close and personal. My uncle Old Dude aka Mr. Fly was someone who never came off as a drug user to me but living with them I was able to see his bad side. He was addicted to heroin, and he couldn't help it. It was an everyday thing for him, and he couldn't fight that addiction. My aunt, on the other hand, his wife was even worse of a drug user than he was. At least my uncle was functional, well at least more functional than she was because she used to get so high that she would pick holes in her skin with scissors because she said it was bugs inside of her. I was freaked the fuck out the first time I saw her do that. She would also fall asleep anywhere. It's been so often that she went to sleep at the most random times. She would fall asleep while she was pulling out of the driveway or at the store or even at a stop light. Her addiction was obvious, and she couldn't hide from it. One time before my mother moved to Atlanta my mother had to come rescue my aunt because me and my cousins were at a store in the parking lot and my aunt was dead ass asleep. My aunt was passed out for hours and she didn't wake up until long after we made it back home. I never understood why she couldn't kick that habit and I'll never get it. It was just hard to watch as a niece of hers and my uncle, but I really felt for my cousins who witnessed those things happen more frequently than I ever did with their parents. It kind of made me grateful for the predicament that I was in because I don't know if I would've been able to deal with having my uncle and aunt as my parents. Watching their addictive habits would've sent me running away from them so long ago. But although my aunt was damn near always high as shit, she loved us. She tried her best to care for us and she was the sweetest woman. I could remember when she was in her normal state of mind. *No one can place judgment on anyone else because you never really know what anyone is going through unless you're walking in their shoes.* But one thing I did know and as far as I could tell, she loved my uncle wholeheartedly and maybe that explains why she was on drugs so badly. She wasn't doing anything but following him and looking up to him. *A man should lead his household in the right way always.* A man is supposed to provide and be there for his woman and steer her in the right direction but in many ways, my uncle steered my aunt in the wrong direction. He was the dope dealer. He was the man who provided the drugs and because he provided the drugs that means his wife got the drugs from him. He made her a heroin addict. He turned her into what she eventually became, which was a junkie. As much love as I have for my uncle who I viewed like a father in my life I know he had flaws and that was his biggest one. But as wrong as he may have been about that I can't say I was an angel like my father viewed me as. Me and my cousins took advantage of my uncle and aunt's addictive tendencies. One of our favorite things to do was to ask them for money when they were high and take money from them when they were asleep. When they were high, they would give us upwards of three hundred dollars just to go to the corner store. It was crazy how much money they had but money was not a problem for my family, especially the older I got. My cousins and I were the bike crew of the neighborhood and everybody on the block knew not to fuck with us because of who my uncle was. We were the popular kids. We stayed with designer on, so they thought we were the cool kids. With the kids in our neighborhood seeing my uncle with the flyest cars, they just thought my cousins and I were the shit. We used to take all the kids to the store with all the money that my uncle and aunt had given to us and let them buy the stuff that they wanted. But eventually, we didn't have to even come out of pocket and spend a dime of the money that we had because the man who owned the store and his workers would just let us get whatever we wanted without paying because of who my uncle was. I'm sure he had a tab at the store from us, but it didn't matter to us because we would get whatever we wanted from there for free. I remember that store because they sold the best deep-dish pizza I could remember. That store was my go-to store because they had the best barbecue chips, pickled eggs, hot sausages, and pickles and I loved the red Faygo Pop they sold. It was like I was living my best life once again learning how not to value a dollar. It's crazy because even when we didn't have to spend our money anymore at that store, I still found a way to spend the money that I had by buying junk food or other crap because money wasn't cherished in my eyes. It wasn't any reason to keep any money that I had because the money came to me like I was the princess of a rich king which in hood terms I was. Even up until now, I have always been very loose with money. I learned that from my uncle who was reckless with money even worse than I was because he had this big marble dining room table that he paid thousands for. In the past, I remember we would come down and see tons of drugs and money with a bunch of his workers sitting around it. I honestly think he should have kept that out of his home where the kids were at, but he clearly didn't see any problems with it. There's no way that my mother didn't know about my uncle's ways which explains why she didn't want me there in the first place. I know that one of my uncle's workers was my aunt's nephew and he was coming over to work but really, he was just over there to finger me on the sofa under a cover. Don't ask me where my uncle or my aunt was to take notice of this sick ass man doing this to me because every time, he did that to me they were nowhere to be found. He knew what he was doing, and he knew when to do what he was doing. I didn't tell anyone because it felt good, it felt like love or maybe I was just too young and too grown for my age at that time. Regardless of what it was, I know that it was wrong. I know for a fact if my uncle knew about any of it, he would have shot his ass right in the face in front of everyone just to send a message to anyone around him to keep their fuckin hands off of his niece. My uncle was the most functional drug user I knew of. Although he was high, he was up on his feet moving with that playa walk smelling like leather and money. He kept some fly shit on. He didn't play about his shoehorns in his shoes or his shoeshine. He also kept us fresh as hell. Whenever he took us on a mall run or whatever place he took us to go shopping it was a shopping spree for everyone. The money for him was just pouring in like water. Back then I loved to hit up Blockbuster and get all the cotton candy and snacks and movies that I wanted and believe me I never had to ask I just had to grab whatever I wanted, and it would be bought. We would also go to the drive-in Movie Theater to kick back and relax and watch a good movie. But as nonchalant as my uncle was with money, one thing that I can say about him is that he did teach us valuable lessons. I can honestly say he didn't play about being a disciplinarian to us especially when we got out of line. He had a Mazda Millennium when they first came out and the cd disc changer was in the trunk, and I jammed it being foolish and just playing around. That was the very first time I experienced my uncle's bad side. He beat the shit out of me that day and I still think about that ass-whooping till this day because of how much it hurt me. I stayed in the closet that whole day because I was too terrified to see his face again. Also, when it came to personal hygiene and cleaning up around the house, he didn't play that shit. He taught me how to wash myself correctly and cross my legs. Certain key points to being a woman. But on the other hand, he and my aunt were very loose about a lot of things especially when they got high, they would be in the room butt-ass naked sleep. I think that messed me up because I once thought it was cool to walk around my kids naked. It's very inappropriate and it leads to the kids being curious or loose as well. It's not something I ever thought was a bad thing to do because I witnessed it so much with my uncle and aunt that summer, I just thought it was normal especially when I was a kid.

Addiction never left my family and it is the reason why my favorite uncle Old Dude, his wife, and my favorite cousin all passed away. My aunt died in 2000 from a drug overdose. *My cousin died in 2016 of a drug overdose and my favorite uncle died in 2018 of a drug overdose. If that's not crazy I'll tell you what's fucked up, my cousin died in the same apartment that my uncle died in, and they both were found dead the same way. My uncle was on his knees in a prayer position. My other favorite cousin who is still alive not only found her mother dead in 2000 but she found her sister dead sixteen years later. I know that she's traumatized by what she had to witness. I know it mentally ruined her because it's fucked me up until now because even though my uncle and aunt were drug addicts, I never thought that they would die because of it. It's hard to witness something over and over as a child and not grow up to fall for that same trap. My girl cousin who ended up overdosing in 2016 used to always say she would never end up like her mother. But with time, life happens, and she ended up falling down that same path which ended her life. Life is so fucked up.* But with that being said, going back to that summer as it was coming to an end my mother was calling and calling my father so she could come and get me. Once she found out that I was at my uncle's home it only took hours for her to end up in Detroit at my uncle's front door picking me up and taking me away from them. I know that whatever conversation was had between my mother and father on that day wasn't a good one at all. That day still sticks in my head because my cousins and I were on our bikes riding with our crew. It was a laundry mat at the end of the street that we were chilling at before I cut through the backyard of my uncle's home where I had seen my mom's car at the end of the street and when she seen us, she came flying down the street. I knew the party was over. I was heartbroken, I did not want to go back to Atlanta but what choice did I have? The whole time I was there at my uncle's house when my mother would call, I would take the phone off of the hook so she wouldn't talk to my uncle or aunt. The entire time she thought that was my dad's home but me taking the phone off of the hook stopped her from finding out it was actually my uncle's house until my dad finally told her the truth. Honestly, me doing that just seems like I'd been running away my whole life. I kind of blacked out once my mom saw me on my bike and she hurried over to get me. I don't remember exactly what happened, but I know that she took me, and we went back to Atlanta leaving my cousins behind. I was so torn because I knew that my mother needed me, but I knew that the love that I needed would never come from her. Instead, it came from my uncle and my aunt along with my cousins. They became the most important family to me way more than my mother ever was. *You can't pick and choose who you're related to, but you can pick and choose who you become close to and that was definitely my uncle, aunt, and their children.* They became the family I've always needed but my mother ripped them away from my life when she took me back to Atlanta. I would say that was the beginning of even worse things to come my way. Leaving my uncle and aunt's house was hard enough but bad news came just weeks after we left Detroit to come back to Atlanta. My uncle Old Dude ended up getting himself into some shit and he got arrested and sent to prison. My mom decided to get my two cousins from my aunt, and they ended up moving in with us in Atlanta. Of course, my aunt Old Dude's wife wasn't in her right frame of mind to keep her kids, so my mom got them. And my aunt stayed in Detroit while she was pregnant with her third child, but she didn't kick her drug abusing habits.

Who could she run to for guidance and help when no one cared to help her? Who can anyone turn to for help with addiction when it's so desperately needed but no one ever seemed to care enough to want to help? But did my aunt ever truly want help or should someone just has stepped up and helped her before it was too late?

Generational Curse #4

Molestation

Molestation is real. Molestation ruins lives and it definitely took a toll on my life way before my adult years. The trip back to Atlanta from Detroit came with terrible consequences for me and my mother, but I would say it was worse for me. My mother was pissed off with me during the whole car ride back to Georgia. It was like I was her enemy just by the way she would glare over at me from time to time. Seems like it was my fault that she fell into a depression and could not take care of me over the summer. She blamed me for my uncle picking me up from the airport and making me stay with him. Even though I had the best summer of my life, I could never tell her my uncle became my favorite person that summer. The drive from

Trapped

Detroit to Atlanta took 11 hours but it felt like forever. My mother maybe uttered a few words to me during the trip and that was either if I needed to use the restroom or if I was hungry and that was it. I felt bad for myself more than anything. I guess being a kid in a kid's world the only thing you think about is yourself and your own happiness. I would sometimes look over at my mother to see the depression on her face. She wasn't happy at all. She wasn't satisfied with anything going on in her life. It was like she was alive but she damn sure wasn't living. Her life must have sucked back then to be alone and depressed. I remember the car ride finally ended when we made it to Atlanta but still, my mother didn't have much to say to me. A few weeks later my mother introduced me to this old man who worked for Kellogg's. I found him a bit strange, but my mother didn't and because I had been feeling kind of bad for her, I was happy that she finally found someone. She seemed happy too but looks can be deceiving. My mother ended up moving us out of our home in Atlanta to Union City, which is a country hick town about thirty minutes outside of Atlanta. The man was still pretty weird to me, but I kept my feelings to myself even as we moved out of our home into his home. He drove an old broken-down pickup truck that was a dusty blue color. He ended up buying my mother a car so that she could drive me and her back and forth to wherever we needed to go. Over some time, my mother began being happier and happier and I must say I liked seeing that. However, I don't think my mother ever truly knew what love was, so she's been searching for it everywhere in all the wrong places I believe her entire life. My mother was beautiful, so her beauty could've attracted a good man into her life, I just believe that it was her terrible choices in men that drove her to choose the wrong kinds of men. This old man seemed to be one of the wrong kinds of men that my mother attracted but I was just a young kid so in my mind I was thinking how could I ever truly know? When we moved into his home it was just him. I don't think that he had any children because in his home he didn't even have any pictures of anyone including himself. I understand being a loner, but he wasn't just a loner, he was creepy as fuck. But what was just as creepy as him was Union City, Georgia. It was country as hell there. There were farms everywhere. It was dirt roads all over the place. The dirt roads were red dirt that I hated with passion. The dirt would stain my expensive shoes and clothes which is why I hated it the most. One thing different between Union City and Detroit is that I grew up being used to seeing liquor stores on every single corner. There was maybe one liquor store in the entire town so it took me a minute to adjust to that. Life in Union City wasn't my cup of tea especially with me knowing that my uncle was arrested by the feds and wasn't expected to get out of prison anytime soon. I thought about him from time to time. Even though he wasn't a saint I know that he was a great person. Those who saw his good side knew that and most of the time I saw his good side. He was compassionate, loving, and caring for the people he loved the most. But I know that he did his dirt in order to get by. *But when you grow up in a world that's against you that doesn't give you many opportunities to succeed you have no choice but to make your own route to making the money* and that's what he did. He hustled and he hustled, and he kept on hustling to the point that the feds got on his ass like white on rice and it was all over from there. *Damn, I miss my uncle Old Dude so much and I miss my favorite cousins too.* I thought about them almost every night as I slept on my bed in my own room at the old man's house. What was odd to me was that the old man and my mother slept in separate rooms, so I really don't know what kind of relationship they had with each other. I just know that the old man did so many things for my mother to make her happy. What kept me sane though was me going to school that fall. I ended up meeting some kids who became my close friends and for my own sanity, I'm glad that I did. I also ended up meeting a really good friend who lived a couple houses up from where I was living, and she had a sister, and her mom and dad were super cool. Her mom would take me to church with them and that was something that I enjoyed. We went to the Martin Luther King Church in Atlanta each and every Sunday and I enjoyed that so much. I always felt love from that family, and I needed it because I damn sure wasn't getting it from home. My mother never knew how to show love to anyone, especially me and I know that I suffered mentally and emotionally because of it. It was around that time my cousins from Detroit moved in with us. Since my uncle Old Dude got arrested and his wife was so much of a drug user that she couldn't take care of her own children. My cousin's moving in with us was probably the best thing to ever happen to me because I began seeing a side of my mother that I had never seen before. She was truly trying to be the best parent she could be. She had us in activities. Me and my girl cousin were cheerleaders and my boy cousin played basketball. It was a great feeling to see my mother finally taking a truly active role in my life as well as the lives of my cousins. I could tell she wanted the very best for us. She somehow became consumed with being a real mother and a caring and loving one at that time because she wanted to be a part of all of our lives so very much. She would always take us to the park to feed the ducks and just play and enjoy our time. *That was my favorite thing to do. I'm more of a nature person which I came to find out as a kid. I love the outdoors and outdoor activities.* Also, my mother had a job, but I don't remember where. One thing that I know is that she never had a stable consistent job, so I don't know where she worked. The man whom we lived with was a complete drunk. He would get off of work and get wasted damn near every day. I can't remember one day going by that he didn't get drunk. It was like he was addicted to getting wasted. I thought he was super cool cause he brought home all the cool cereals and snacks from Kellogg's and he used to give me and my cousins money. My girl cousins hated him. I remember they used to always tell me that he was a weirdo. They never got any good vibes from him. *I didn't know any better and when you don't know any better can you fault someone for not knowing what they probably should know which is don't ever trust a strange man or woman for that matter?* I wish I just saw the signs. I wish I could see the future before the future happened and that way I could've just avoided all of the bullshit that he ended up putting me through. I can't remember when the first time was, or how it started, but the old man started having sex with me. I remember one time he came home and got fucked up and I mean pissy drunk, and my cousins and I were downstairs. He said to me "I brought you some treats home, now it's time for me to get my treats." Just a few minutes later I remember him guiding me to his room and in no time, I didn't have any clothes on. He got naked before I did, and he just began playing with himself right in front of me with no shame whatsoever. His old body was gross to me, but I felt as though I needed some kind of love and affection from someone, and he gave me what I needed. He brought me treats and gave me money and he would tell me how pretty I was often. He would say it in front of my cousins and my mother, so I never felt terrible about betraying my mother. Even though he was an old man, and I was a minor who shouldn't have been having sex in the first place, I was searching for love and affection in the wrong place. That day I got undressed right before his perverted eyes as he continued to play with himself as he watched my underage body. At that time, I didn't find it sickening but reflecting on it now, I know that it was fucked up. He just stretched out on the center of his bed covered in his hairy legs, arms, chest, and pubic area while just watching me remove my panties. I should've known better. I should've been smarter. I should've been wise beyond my age, but unfortunately for me I wasn't. I was mentally fucked up then. I ended up climbing on top of him and watching his eyes roll to the back of his head as he got inside of me. I rode him like a rodeo. Afterward, when it was all said and done, he said to me "Now tomorrow, you get more treats." I ran upstairs and cried to my cousins and told them what had happened. We all sat there and cried together. They were crying about what happened to me, but they were also crying because they missed my uncle and their mom. We were a total wreck. We wept all night long and my mother didn't even come to our rescue. My older female cousin promised me that she would never tell anyone about what I told them just like when I lost my virginity back in Detroit. If I had the mindset I do now back then, I would've told her to tell the police, but I didn't. I just felt like it was the right thing for her to do. In my mind back then my cousin was solid, our secrets remained with us and no one else, and that's what I loved about her in fact about them both. The molestation could've continued if it wasn't for him and his sickening ways. One day me and my cousins watched him burst out of his room butt ass naked trying to come into our room. At that very moment I felt disgusted with myself for feeling that he loved me when really, he just used me for his own sick pleasure. On that day he tried to barge into our room, it was the way he looked and acted that terrified me the most. It was like he was possessed by Satan or something. The way he looked was horrifying. He was old as hell, and he smelt like beer. It was a horrible sight to see. I was fucking disgusted by him at that point. I no longer saw him as the man who was nice to me that gave me treats and sweets whenever I wanted them. Instead, I saw him as the evil devil that he was who took advantage of a young girl. He manipulated me and played with my mind and just fucked me up. I wish that I could've killed him myself. I wish that I had the mental courage to just end his life because he deserved to die by my hands. From that day forward I never let him touch me and he rolled with that because he had no other choice. Still, until this day I will say that I never allowed my pussy to be taken from me without my consent. I was always willing to have sex with him and I guess I was just thinking that it was love or maybe I was just hot as hell. Being real I know that I was just hot as hell. I was too grown for my young age, and I just didn't give a fuck about what anyone thought ever, the problem with that thinking is that it was illegal and still molestation. I continued to go to school and attend my activities. Never once did I tell my mom about his sick ass. So, she never knew.

———

I enjoyed getting up for school because I knew that I was going to get fingered on the school bus by a 12th-grade fine-ass boy that I liked a lot. He had my heart because he looked good to me but deep down, I knew that he didn't like me half as much as I liked him. He was just using me for his sexual pleasure just like the old man. *I had to learn that most men no matter the age, does just that, they use women for their pleasure only.* Back then the school I went to was Bear Creek Middle which sat next door to Creek Side High. So, when the bus came it was middle and high schoolers who took the bus. Looking for love in all the wrong places could be the story of my life. *It's like digging for gold in a place that has no gold, but you keep digging anyway hoping that you will stumble upon pounds of gold.* I wanted love and I just wasn't afraid to search high and low for it, even if it meant me being used by some horny guys to get it. I know that love was coming my way at some point. Eventually, my cousins moved back with their mom to Detroit, and I was back alone which I never wanted or imagined happening once my cousins moved in with us. My cousins were my support system because the Lord knows I didn't have anyone else I could lean on for mental and emotional support. *There I was at a young age battling the world all by myself. Feeling all alone with a mother that never truly loved me. Well, at least that's how I felt.* Me and my mother ended up moving to Marietta and she got us our own place to stay. I know I never told my mother about what the old man did to me, but I guess maybe her motherly intuition knew that taking me away from him was the best thing that she could've done, and believe me I was more than happy that she did that. *I needed my father in my life. I needed his caring and loving touch. I needed someone that I could confide in. I needed someone that I could tell all my problems to that would tell me how it is and not what I wanted to hear. I needed my father to be my dad. I needed his advice and most importantly I just needed him to be there for me to protect me from things like these men and all the times I ended up molested.*

Dear father: "I love you and I appreciate you for giving me life, but I needed you around me more." "I needed you in my presence." "I needed you to be there for me because without you I've been trying to find myself for so long and still till this day Dad, I'm struggling. I have yet to find myself and I still yearn for your love.

L.A TIPS: REMOVING THE BLACK MAN FROM THE HOME TAKES AWAY FROM A CHILD'S GROWTH AND DEVELOPMENT. THE BLACK WOMAN WHO DISRESPECTS AND REBELS AGAINST THE LEADERSHIP AND AUTHORITY

OF THE BLACK MAN IS A DIRECT CAUSE OF THE BREAKDOWN IN OUR FAMILY STRUCTURE. BLACK WOMEN HAVE BEEN TAUGHT THAT IF THE BLACK MAN DOES NOT GIVE MONEY, THEN HE IS NOT A LEADER OF THE HOME, WHICH IT STRIPS THE VALUABLE STRENGTHS OF A MAN WHICH LEADS TO HIM NOT EVER PROVIDING FOR HIS HOME OR HIS CHILDREN.

Generational Curse #5

Teenage Pregnancy

Growing up with no sense of direction, structure, or discipline can leave anyone lost in the world and I'm no exception to that rule either. Generational curses, tend to hold a hefty winning percentage in the lives of so many families and in my family, it may be undefeated unless I finally step up and defeat it. But way back then in my teenage years, my family's generational curses were whooping my ass in ways that I can't even describe. Life is hard I know but why in the world has it been so difficult on me is my only question! I was just fourteen years old, and I had experienced a life rougher than most could ever imagine, and it only goes downhill from there. I mean where the hell is the balance? From my favorite uncle going to the feds to my father being more of an absentee father who probably cares more about the street life than my life. My mother went from being a loveless parent to being the most passionate mother ever when my cousins moved in with us. That love vanished the very second my cousins went back to Detroit. Once again, I'm just a lonely little girl in a world filled with so many people but I feel alone. I don't know who I can turn to in my time of need. I'm searching for love, but love must be avoiding me because I can't find it. I thought I found it in the old man who gave me candy and money. I thought I found it in the guy who played with me in the back of the school bus every morning. I keep thinking I'm finding it but I'm just searching for love in all the wrong places. My mother and I ended up moving from that country hick town over to Marietta. It was nothing but Mexicans and burritos on the street we moved on, Franklin Road. I can't lie I hated it but with every downside comes some sort of upside and the upside was that my mother and me moved into a two-bedroom apartment. I didn't waste much time adapting to my new city because I ended up filling out a few applications for some jobs and in no time, I got a call from McDonalds who hired me right away. The job came and ended just like a bad relationship. I lied on my job application about my age so that I could get the job and somehow, they found out that I wasn't old enough to work there. I was fourteen just searching for a positive way out of the negative life I was forced into but somehow, I just kept getting pulled back into it. That job was supposed to keep me occupied from all of the bullshit that my life was used to, but I guess when the devil works hard to grab a hold of your life and fuck it up, he sometimes succeeds. Well, he succeeded with me over and over again and that time was no different. I know the kind of person I am, and I am someone who wanted love and I kept looking for love in all of the wrong places. The job was more to occupy my free time and to keep me from doing some of the things I'd been doing. As pissed off as I was with losing my McDonalds job, I just felt something inside of me telling me not to give up, so I didn't. I let some time go by before I decided to restart my job search and to my surprise, there were some jobs out there for a young fourteen-year-old. I ended up getting a job at Harry's Farmers Market in the seafood department scaling fish. My work didn't interfere with my school schedule at all. I still attended school, and everything went well at first. But I noticed that my mom didn't seem so happy with whatever she had going on. I would've thought that us moving away from that old creepy man into a home of our own would've brought some joy to my mother's life, but it didn't. She was just angry with life or whatever was going on in her life at that time and she damn sure took her anger out on me. I know that I got most of the beatings I ever received from her in that apartment. She was just always angry like the devil just took control over her especially whenever I was around her, maybe she was just plain old sick of my shit because she knew I was headed to destruction. I know that she wanted love. I know that she felt all alone just like I did. It was like we were two distant strangers living in the same house. We both didn't know how to show each other any kind of love. For some reason, my mother signed me up for the Boys and Girls Club and I hated it. I could tell it was around that time that I was starting to become very rebellious, so I started to go against anything she said. It was like I just had enough of all her bullshit. I should've been shown love by the only person that was always there in my life. I should've been consoled when I was upset and picked up whenever I fell down, but she never did any of that for me. I guess when you feel like you're being neglected for so long you begin to rebel and trust me I began to rebel. She would tell me don't go outside and I still did. I didn't care to listen to her even though I would get caught every single time by her. I felt neglected and I was searching for love but mainly affectionate love from someone and I mean probably anyone. It's human nature to crave love no matter who you are. You can be the biggest pimp in the world or the nerdiest girl ever and you still want to feel affectionate love from someone that you care for. Hell, sometimes it doesn't even have to be someone that you care for it can be anyone. But with my age came hormones and puberty, so sex became a big craving of mine, especially after I experienced it already. Honestly, sex probably started to become the most important thing that I cared about at that time because that's the only thing that felt good as far as affectionate love goes to me. I guess it's just what I wanted back then. It's what I needed, and I needed it badly. At first the Mexican guys in my neighborhood never really paid me much attention but I guess they could sense that I was hot, so they began to hit on me. I didn't pay them much attention, but they were constantly trying to flirt with me. "Hey Mami!" I know that it was only one thing that they wanted from me and honestly, after some time it was all that I wanted from them.

Eventually, something went down. It was an older short Mexican guy that smelled like beans that somehow caught my attention. Not much time went by before we started having sex. It wasn't memorable at all. Just really something to do. It's nothing that I would ever gossip about. Any sex at that time especially at my age should've been something that I enjoyed, but at that time I was way too experienced, so I knew good sex from bad sex, and this was very bad sex. Come to think about it, I never really felt anything. It literally felt like I laid down and someone was just on top of me. The heavy breathing coming from him and the joy on his face showed me that it was good to him. But the dissatisfaction on my face showed that the sex didn't mean a damn thing to me. I remember leaving his house a little after I came from school, and I just felt so disgusted with myself once again like the old creepy man. I made sure that only happened with him that one time and never again. I was living too fast for my own good because I was looking for something more enjoyable. And clearly. I thought I was grown, so I could do whatever I wanted to do with my body. I remember coming home one day after I left the Boys and Girls Club. I wasn't happy at all about my mother forcing me to go, but I went, and I know not as often as she thought I was going. That one evening though I ran into a guy who lived down the hallway from my apartment building. He was tall and dark-skinned and caught my attention and by the looks on his face I know I caught his too. He couldn't take his eyes off me. I even looked back at him a couple of times after I passed by him standing in his doorway shirtless. Damn I was way too grown for my age because the thoughts that were in my mind at that time should've never been in my mind the moment, I saw him. He licked his lips at me as he watched me take my house keys out of my pocket. I could hear the sound of footsteps coming in my direction which caused me to turn around only to see him standing just a few feet away from me with that charming smile on his face. That smile had me hooked right then and there and I knew that whatever he wanted to do with me I would allow him to do it and that's just what happened. I know that he was much older than me, but I didn't care. He must've known that I was way younger than him but based on how he looked at me I knew he didn't care. It all started on that night. We began having sex all over his apartment and we did it for months. We had sex everywhere in his home including the bathroom, his bedroom, his living room, and all over his kitchen. I mean when we fucked, he made me forget about all of my problems. I couldn't think about anything besides getting a couple of orgasms and he made sure of that. I know that he didn't love me, it was all just sex, but it was fine because I didn't love him either. For me, it was what he thought it was, and nothing more than that. It was all lust and love just didn't exist between the two of us. But as good as the sex was with him, I still had plenty of issues that I was dealing with. Mentally I wasn't stable at all. I knew back then that my head was messed up. I was so torn mentally that one day I just decided to take a sharp knife to school. I swear to myself that I wasn't trying to hurt anyone but for some reason, I felt the need to bring that knife with me. I heard so many girls in the school hallways talk about how this guy tried to force themselves on them or how that guy forced themselves inside of them. Hearing those constant conversations with other girls just from a distance when I wasn't even a part of those conversations brought some worry to me. I couldn't help but think about that old man who my mother, cousins and I used to live with, and I could only think about what if. What if he one day showed up to my school to hunt me down? What if he saw me walking home from school one day and he caught up to me and kidnapped me? With all of the bullshit I was already going through in my life paranoia wasn't supposed to be added to the list, but it was. So, because it got added to my list of already a ton of bullshit going on, I had to bring that knife with me every day to and from school. I got beyond comfortable with bringing that knife with me every day to the point that I began to become a little reckless with me keeping that knife hidden from everyone. I would just pull it out as I stood before my locker and just shove it into my locker until the end of school. I knew that sometimes the security would come to random classrooms to do security checks and I didn't want to get caught with that sharp knife in my possession. But I should've moved smarter because one day someone saw me putting that knife into my locker. Within that hour the police were ripping off my locker door where they found it and I was being sent down to the principal's office to answer questions about why did I have that knife in my possession. I didn't have any answers for the principal, and I damn sure didn't have any answers for my mother who showed up hours after the principal called her to come and pick me up from school. I got expelled from school and I was placed in an alternative school. *Sometimes everything in life that may seem bad just isn't so bad after all.*

Me going to an alternative school probably was the best thing that happened to me at that time. I loved that school because it seemed like the schoolwork was so much easier and there were far fewer people at that school than at my old school. I'm a loner so that was right up my alley. I ended up meeting a Caucasian girl there that was super cool, and she was really laid back just like me. Her name was Cassidy, and she was my dawg. She was such a cool person and she made going to school fun for me. I had someone to hang out with now daily unlike at my old school and I must say I liked that. I mean everyone needs friends or just a friend and Cassidy was that friend that I needed, and I believe she needed me just as much. We both were misfits who didn't try to fit in with the so-called in crowd. We were just cool girls that just liked having fun and living life and that's exactly what we did. One thing about my mom though is if I wanted to go to a friend's house, she would let me go. I don't know if she just wanted to just get rid of me or what, but it seemed like she didn't give a damn. She just always allowed me to go and hang out with my friend and that's exactly what I did with Cassidy. I was living the life of a grown woman at just fourteen years old; it might have felt like a good thing for me at that time because I was young, dumb and filled with sexual desires, but it wasn't a good thing for me at all as I would soon find out. Cassidy's mom lived in Chamblee, Georgia and we would go over there to hangout and have a good old time. It was so much freedom because if I'm not mistaken her mom was on drugs and she dated an old man who was taking care of her. Cassidy had a couple of sisters and the shit they were doing I shouldn't have been there to see but I saw it repeatedly. They were always taking ecstasy pills. They would get high out of their mind, and I would just watch. I couldn't believe my eyes and how open they were and just careless about taking drugs in front of me. Cassidy wasn't Mrs. Innocent at all because she was right there with her sisters' popping pills and snorting cocaine, right in front of me. It was something she was used to doing and I refused to do it even though I was tempted to just try it out. Hell, for some reason there's always that one day when a person just lets their hair down and just lives life like there's no tomorrow and that's exactly what I thought about doing but I just didn't have it in me to do it. One night though Cassidy's sisters took us to the Crystal Palace, and I was in there without a drug in my system looking at all the crazy shit that was going on. My friend was getting high and everybody else there too, but me. I can honestly say I never tried a drug as a kid and Cassidy never offered me any. She was my best friend at that time, and I loved her spirit even though she was a pill popper. Cassidy and I were super cool always and I still to this day miss her. She loved my company and I loved hers and we just always had great times together. We went to all of the parties in Marietta and Atlanta because she damn near knew everyone. And even though I wasn't of legal age I was getting into clubs without ever worrying about showing any id. But the path that I was going down wasn't a good one and my mom saw that from a million miles away. Hanging out with Cassidy became my thing to do after school so surely, I stopped going to the Boy and Girls Club. I guess the people over there must've called my mother to tell her because one day I showed up home after 9pm and I saw my mother sitting in the living room across from a lady. My mom got me a big sister who was supposed to be something like a mentor for me. I remember my big sister ended up getting me a phone and my mom took it from me and used it for her own personal use. What I thought was going to be a terrible experience ended up being a good one for me because my big sister was hood. She was like a gangster who knew how and when to show her gangster side and I loved it. In front of my mom, she was a sweet angel but alone with me she was a gangster who treated me like her little sister that she cared for so much. She taught me so much about life and how to deal with people. She would always give me tips and pointers on how a young lady should move out in the real world and I must say I loved her advice. I took mental notes on everything she told me. She was in my corner, and I loved it. It was a constant thing for her to just pick me up and take me out on outings where she would just talk to me about life and how to deal with it. But like all the good things that come into my life, it didn't last. The last thing I remember her saying was "I should appreciate my mom because I had the best bed." I was confused, but I assume she like my bed. It was nice, it had mirrors and lights and marble or something around it. I used to stick gum on the top of the bedhead because like so many other things in my life I just didn't appreciate it or value it. I should've been taught to value everything that I had instead of basically being taught to take everything for granted like whatever comes stays forever when really it can all be taken away at the drop of a hat. Something I would say about my mother now that I probably didn't appreciate back then is that no matter what she always made sure that I had a nice bedroom set and fly-ass clothes, but as I start rebelling against her getting those nice things stopped. It's like she noticed that I was being ungrateful, and she punished me by no longer gifting me things. I wasn't that cute little girl anymore to her. She may have thought that if she stopped giving me things, which would change me for the better, but it only made matters worse. Her plan blew up in her face because I only began rebelling against her more and more. One evening I took my mother's car to bring the trash to the garbage bin that was located way in the front of the apartment complex. My mother ended up calling the police on me and that's where the divide between my mother and me truly started in my eyes. I could never see things from her perspective, and she could never see things from mine. I was just bad as hell. I'm guessing she probably thought that I took her car out to run away, but I just went to take the trash out, which wasn't even right. I just wanted to drive around for a little, but she wasn't having any of it. That day when she called the cops on me and almost had me arrested was the day, I knew that me and my mother would never ever get along. It was like on that day she truly became my enemy or at least that's how I painted the image of her in my mind. I didn't want to be around her anymore, so I just decided to run away from home. Eventually, Cobb police found me and put me in juvenile detention for 30 days. By that time, I was mischievous. I got out and continued to go to school until one day me and a girl in my apartment building decided to go out with these two older guys. Of course, we lied about our age, and they took us to a hotel room to have sex. They fucked us like we were sluts. They treated us like two-dollar prostitutes on the corner and I can't believe I tolerated that. They ran a train on us both. Like I said I was living the life of a grown careless woman when I was just 14 years old. My friend and I got caught by my mother and we ended up telling on the guys who had sex with us. I guess my friend and I both panicked. She knew that if her mother found out what she had been doing she probably would've been sent away to live with her grandparents somewhere in Mississippi and I knew that the possibilities of me ending back up in juvenile detention were high, so we decided that it was either going to be our asses or theirs and we of course chose them to get fucked over. We told on the two men, and they got locked up for having sex with minors. I remember when I got home my mother didn't say a word to me, she just pointed to my bedroom, and I knew to head straight there. But I heard the sound of her running over at me causing me to look back at her and then her fist punched my face over and over again. She knocked me down on the floor as I tried to cover my face, but she kept hitting me and she knocked my ass out right in front of my bedroom door. She dragged my unconscious body right next to my bed and just left me there resting on the cold floor. I woke up hours later with a pounding headache and feeling sick to my gut. I'm guessing that hell of an ass whopping my mother had given me was supposed to be my wake-up call to get me from going down the dark road that I was heading on that she could see a mile away, but it wasn't. In fact, her doing what she did only caused me to remove my seatbelt, press harder on the gas pedal and head faster down that dark road than ever before. I was on a road of destruction and my mother knew that she was losing control of me. I was already headed down a dark and dangerous path at that point and truly I don't think there is anyone alive who could've stopped my fate. One thing though that I must say is that I didn't see once since we moved to Marietta was my mom bringing men into our home. But it was an African guy who lived in the back of the apartment building that she was cool with. He used to cook for us, but we mostly went to his place. He and his sister lived together. They were always trying to talk some sense into me, but I didn't listen. My mother must've told them about the path that I was on because they would always try to preach to me, but I wasn't trying to listen to their sermon, plus I never understood what he was saying. My mother was just like me or better, yet I was just like my mother searching for love in all of the wrong places. My mother jumped from man to man trying to find love and it just seemed like love was never her destiny and it probably will never be mine either. My mother and I were always an incomplete family. My father was living his own life and my mother was searching like a madwoman in the dark without a flashlight for Mr. Perfect, but he was nowhere to be found. While she was searching for love I was doing the same thing. I ended up pregnant as a teenage mother to be and the last thing I wanted to do was tell my mother that I was pregnant. I eventually told her, and she blew a gasket of rage at me for falling down that path that she desperately wanted me to avoid. Life was just hitting my mother with haymakers from all directions. It was just so much all around the same time from her best friend being shot; on top of that my aunt who is my favorite uncle's wife had just died of a heroin overdose and it was a lot to deal with. My mother broke the news to me at the worst possible time when I told her that I was pregnant. Did she tell me that to stress me out to the point that I had a miscarriage, or did she tell me that then because she knew that was the best time to tell me? I was angry with her for telling me that news so far after my aunt passed away. I couldn't look my mother in the eyes, especially when she told me that she wasn't going to allow me to go to the funeral. I couldn't believe what I heard from her and that just pissed me off even more with her. I was over the whole situation with her and with just everything going on in general at that point. So, what did I do? I just ran away again as it was the only thing that I could think of doing.

Life is an unexpected journey of ups and downs no one can ever anticipate what is coming next. Is good coming or is bad coming? I guess you'll just have to wait and find out. The problem is that you will find out when it's too late or you'll find out just in time. For me, it's always been when it's too late filled with a bunch of bullshit on top of more bullshit.

To Be Continued!!!!

Trapped: Finding my Way out of Generational Curses Part 2 Coming Soon…

Author Bio

"Trapped" is a book series that narrates my life story. We all have a unique story to tell, but I am courageous enough to share mine regardless of any judgment I may receive. Like many of us, I have experienced some form of trauma in my past. Fortunately, I was able to recognize and confront the traumas in my life and understand their root causes. Through my book series, I aim to break down my story and explore each generational curse that has affected my family.

My decision to share my story comes from the belief that it can help others who are struggling with fear, reality, or judgment. Sharing our stories is a critical part of the healing process. Moreover, I have found that many people do not know how to break free from generational curses. By learning from my experiences, readers can overcome tough obstacles in their own lives and make positive changes.

Lanesha Allen lives in Gwinnett County, GA is from Detroit Michigan, and is currently a caregiver. Lanesha has 7 more books to come…

Contact Lanesha @ laneshaallen@yahoo.com

Website: laneshaallen.com

Interested in Writing and/or Publishing a Book?

Visit a2zbookspublishing.net